Collins

Revised Tune In!

Master Your Listening and Speaking Skills

Adheres to National Education Policy – FOUNDATIONAL STAGE

Author: Safa Abdul Razak | **Series Editor:** Dr K Padmini Shankar

Preface

Revised Tune In! is an innovative listening and speaking course that is closely aligned with the National Education Policy, 2020. The course consists of eight books for Classes 1 to 8 with their accompanying audio-visual resources.

Aims

The main aim of *Revised Tune In!* is to help students gain communicative competence in using English in the real world by developing the key aural and oral skills. It aids to boost confidence in learners to develop fluency in using English in academic, personal and social contexts. It uses a step-by-step interactive approach with experiential tasks based on 21st century skills to help learners listen, understand and respond appropriately.

The number of chapters ranges from 10 to 13 in each level. Each chapter is built around a theme and focuses on specific language and communicative functions related to it. Special focus is also given on enriching the fund of context-specific vocabulary and spoken grammar, along with the use of correct pronunciation, intonation, stress and pause.

The chapters are structured to include the following sections:

Learning objectives defines language learning goals at the beginning of each chapter.

Getting started introduces the theme in an engaging way.

Listening and learning includes focused listening activities that help learners develop active listening skills, scan for details and draw inferences from what they have heard.

Speaking and practising has focused speaking activities that help learners develop fluency and accuracy in speaking, and hone their presentation skills.

Saying it right covers different aspects of phonics and pronunciation.

Word Wizard provides vocabulary support in the form of key words and phrases required for the task.

Grammar Guide provides language and grammar inputs to facilitate accurate language production.

Manners matter! contain gestural and verbal clues that are vital for making the right impression while speaking.

Info byte provides quick tips and tricks about sounds and spoken language.

Interacting and communicating includes integrated listening and speaking tasks; usually interactive pair and group work for students to practise and assess what they have learnt.

Fun Activity contains activities for enjoyment while learning. Each book also has the following special features:

Dictation time provides additional practice for the learners' listening and spelling skills.

Take a break! are three well-designed activities that allow learners to refresh the topics learnt in the preceding chapters.

Saying it better! teaches common phrases and guides learners to avoid incorrect and colloquial language usage.

Children's Literary Fest is an art-integrated activity that focuses on increasing the learners' interest in literature.

How to use the book

Each chapter is based on a theme and focuses on a communicative function. Parents and teachers can initiate the learners into the theme of the chapter through the warm-up activity given in *Getting started*.

Chapter

Draw the student's attention to the learning objectives given at the beginning of the chapters. This would help them to focus on the key learning points of the chapter.

Do the listening and learning activities for developing active listening skills. Play the audio tracks at least twice for 'while-listening' and 'post-listening' tasks. During the first time, the students should be asked only to listen. When they listen to it for the second time, get them to complete the task. Give them clear instructions at the beginning of the tasks and check whether they understand what needs to be done.

Conduct the phonic drills and pronunciation activities with care. Get the students to listen and repeat the words and phrases multiple times till they get the pronunciation right. While this can be done as a class activity too, it would be best to monitor each student individually. Use the audio-visual input to learn the right way of making the English sounds.

When conducting the speaking activities, make sure all the students get a fair chance to participate. Demonstrate the task and check whether the students know how to do it. The presentation tips given for the activities in the *Manners matter!* boxes can be used to inculcate good habits and to build the right attitude required in students to make an impression when they speak.

For Assessment

Teachers can choose any of the listening and speaking activities for testing the students' achievement levels. It is, however, advisable to share the parameters of assessment with the students beforehand so that they know what is expected of them. Teachers can refer to the Teacher's Resource Books for this.

Teacher's Resource Books contain the lesson plans, teaching strategies and the answer keys besides the parameters of assessment for each task.

DigiSuite, the interactive digital resource pack, has the e-book with audio for the listening tasks, interactive activities and training videos demonstrating the right way of doing the speaking tasks.

We hope that teachers and students would find this series useful in developing listening and pronunciation and speaking skills and that it would enable students to become effective communicators in English.

Key to NEP tags and SDG icons

Revised Tune In! is a listening and speaking course that is closely aligned with the National Education Policy, 2020. It uses interactive approach, and experiential activities to build communicative competence in students. This series aims to prepare learners with the various skills outlined in the National Education Policy, 2020.

These skills have been tagged appropriately for the user's convenience. Here is the key to the tags.

India Focus NEP

- India Focus puts spotlight on the heritage, culture, customs, and history and geography of the Indian subcontinent.
- This provides students a deeper understanding of their homeland and creates a sense of solidarity.

Art Integration NEP

- Art Integrated Learning (AIL) is a teaching-learning model that integrates fine arts (painting, sculpture, architecture, music, and poetry), performing arts (theatre and dance), and photography with teaching new concepts.
- This provides students with an experiential and a multi-disciplinary learning experience.

Cross-curricular NEP

- The cross-curricular approach to a topic recognizes that all subjects are interlinked. It includes contributions from several different disciplines or viewpoints for effective learning.
- Certain activities cover cross-curricular content appropriate to that class.

Happiness Content NEP

- Learning should be an enjoyable process for learners. It should focus on building and understanding new concepts rather than rote learning.
- Children should experience happiness through learning and awareness, active participation in class, and also in their relationships with their friends and family.

Experiential Learning NEP

- Experiential learning is a process of learning through hands-on experience. Here, students 'learn by doing' an activity followed by reflective observation on the experience from multiple perspectives.
- This method helps learners link existing knowledge to understand new concepts and apply it to make decisions.

Twenty-First Century Skills

- The twenty-first century skills ensure that today's students can thrive in an ever-changing world and can use these skills to learn constantly.
- Here are the most commonly cited twenty-first century skills in this series:

Critical Thinking NEP

Communication Skills NEP

Collaboration NEP

Creativity NEP

Digital Literacy NEP

Sustainable Development Goals

- The Sustainable Development Goals, adopted by the United Nations in 2015, are a collection of 17 interlinked global goals designed to achieve a better and more sustainable future for all by 2030.
- Here are the 17 goals:

Detailed Contents

Chapter	Listening and learning	Speaking and practising	Saying it right & Dictation time	Interacting and communicating	Fun Activity
1. **When we meet, we greet.** (*Communicative functions:* formal greetings and leave taking; introducing oneself)	Listening to conversations and choosing the correct option; matching the pictures correctly and filling gaps	*Pair work:* role-playing a conversation, introducing oneself to the partner	Practising words with consonant sounds *n*, *p*, *s*, *t* and vowel sound *a*; practising a rhyme focusing on the sounds taught Listening and writing words	*Group work:* greeting friends as per the time of the day	*Group work:* playing Catch the greeting ball game
2. **Hello! My name is Raman.** (*Communicative functions:* talking about oneself, expressing one's likes and dislikes)	Listening to conversations for details and filling gaps; matching the pictures correctly	*Pair work:* talking about oneself and one's likes and dislikes	Listening to a poem and singing along; practising words with consonant sounds *c*, *d*, *h*, *m*, *r* and vowel sound *i* Listening and writing words	Listening to people talking about themselves and filling gaps; telling the teacher about one's likes and dislikes	Solving a riddle and colouring the correct picture
3. **This is my home.** (*Communicative functions:* talking about one's family and home; describing people)	Listening to conversations for details and answering questions; listening and colouring pictures	*Pair work:* talking about one's family members; talking about one's house	Practising words with consonant sounds *g*, *l*, *f*, *b*, and vowel sounds *a* and *i*; identifying words with the same sound Listening and writing words	Asking and answering questions based on the given picture	Making a family tree
Take a break!					
4. **This is my friend.** (*Communicative functions:* describing people and talking about their physical features)	Listening to conversations for details and answering questions and matching items	*Pair work:* describing one's friends and classmates	Practising words with consonant sounds *l*, *m* and *p*, and vowel sound *e* Listening and writing words	Describing one's friends and neighbours; listening and reporting what one heard	Finding descriptive words in a wordsearch
5. **This is my classroom.** (*Communicative functions:* describing things; making polite requests and asking for permission)	Listening to a description of a school and matching the correct options; filling gaps	*Pair work:* describing one's school playground; asking for permission based on the given pictures	Practising words with consonant sounds *r*, *s*, *t* and vowel sounds *e* and *a* Listening and writing words	Describing things around us by talking about their shape, colour and size; asking teacher's permission	Spotting differences in two identical pictures

Chapter	Listening and learning	Speaking and practising	Saying it right & Dictation time	Interacting and communicating	Fun Activity
6. I have a pet. (*Communicative functions:* describing actions using the *-ing* form of verbs)	Listening to conversations for details and choosing the correct option; listening to a class in progress and writing the names of wild and pet animals	*Group work:* asking for information and answering questions; listening and talking about how to take care of pets	Practising words with consonant sounds *s, t, n, p* and vowel sound *i*; identifying words ending with the same sound Listening and writing words	*Group work:* talking about a pet and how to take care of it; looking at a picture and answering the questions	*Group work:* playing a game on animal sounds
		Take a break!			
7. I like to dance and play. (*Communicative functions:* expressing our likes and dislikes)	Listening to conversations for details and marking the correct answer; choosing the correct option to answer questions	Talking about what one likes and doesn't like to eat; making a list	Practising words having consonant blends with *ck, m, d,* and practising vowel sound *o*; looking at the pictures and identifying the sounds Listening and writing words	Answering questions about one's likes and dislikes; listening to a conversation and choosing the correct answer	Colouring the things one likes
8. I feel happy. (*Communicative functions:* expressing feelings and needs; accepting and rejecting an offer politely)	Listening to conversations for details, and matching the sentences; identifying the correct objects	*Pair work:* offering food or drinks; talking about how one is feeling	Practising words with consonant sounds *y, w* and *z* and practising vowel sounds *o* and *i* Listening and writing words	Listening and identifying the correct object; *group-work:* ordering food at a restaurant	Listening to a song and singing along
9. Where is my schoolbag? (*Communicative functions:* listening to and following directions; asking for and giving directions)	Listening to a conversation and following the directions on a map; matching sentences correctly	*Pair work:* giving directions to different places in one's school; practising the given dialogue	Practising words with consonant sounds *d, g, n, p, t* and vowel sound *u* Listening and writing words	Looking at the pictures and describing the position of things; talking about where one keeps one's favourite things	Listening to a song and doing the actions
		Take a break!			
10. What is the time now? (*Communicative functions:* describing the weather, telling the time and talking about one's daily routine)	Listening to conversations and filling gaps to complete statements and choosing the correct option	*Pair work:* talking about the weather; talking about the time one wakes up at on a Sunday	Practising words with consonant sounds *g* and *n* and vowel sounds *o* and *u* Listening and writing words	Listening to a conversation and arranging the pictures in the correct order; *group work:* talking about one's daily routine; looking at the pictures and talking about the weather	Matching the actions with the time one does them
11. I can dance. (*Communicative functions:* talking about what one can or cannot do; asking for permission using *can*)	Listening to conversations for details and identifying the correct pictures and choosing the correct actions	*Pair work:* talking about what one can and cannot do; talking about a unique ability one has	Practising words with the long and short vowel sounds *i* and *o* Listening and writing words	*Group work:* asking questions to friends and filling in a table	Listening and repeating a poem
		Saying it better!			
		Children's Literary Fest			

Contents

1 When we meet, we greet.

In this chapter, we will:

- listen and learn to greet properly.
- listen and learn to introduce ourselves.
- learn to say words beginning with consonant sounds n, p, s, t and practise vowel sound a.

Getting started

Happiness Content NEP

A. *Sing* 1.1

Listen to the song and sing along.

Good morning | Good afternoon | Good evening | Good night

Listening and learning

B1. *Listen* 1.2

Listen to Arjun and Rima. They are talking about greetings.

B2. *Sort* 1.3

Listen to Arjun and Rima again. Which greetings can be said at any time when we meet someone? Colour the right stars.

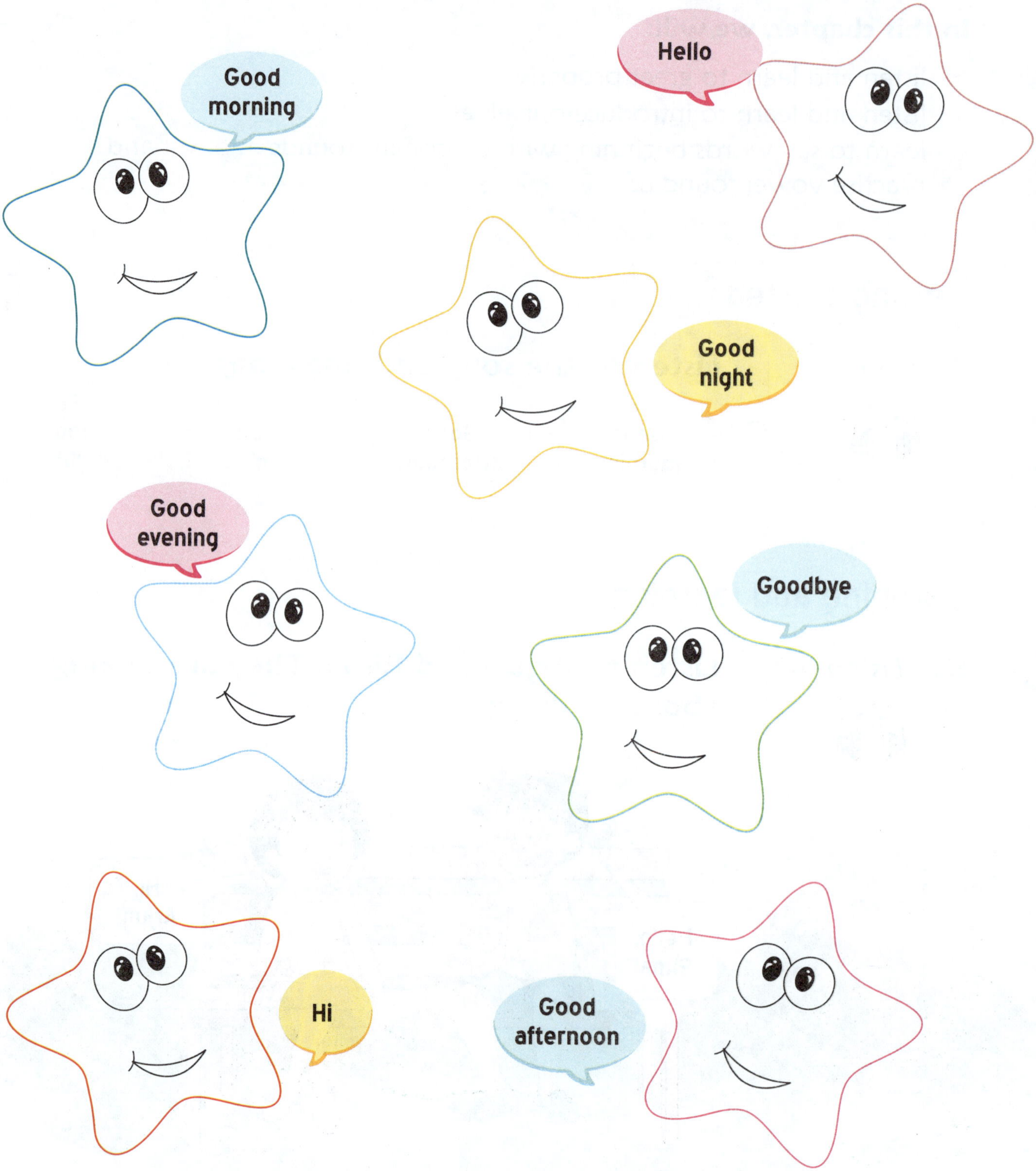

B3. *Match*

Listen to the people greet others. Draw lines to match the people and their greetings.

1

2

3

Good morning

Good night

Hello

Good evening

Goodbye

Good afternoon

4

5

6

B4. *Gap-fill*

Priya and Manav are meeting for the first time. Listen to them. Then, fill in the blanks.

Speaking and practising

Communication Skills NEP

C. *Introduce*

Work in pairs. Role-play this conversation with your partner.

Tina: Hello! My name is Tina.

Arvind: Hello, Tina! My name is Arvind.
Nice to meet you.

Tina: Nice to meet you too, Arvind.

Now, greet each other and tell your name in the same way.

A: Hello! My name is ....

B: Hello, ... !
My name ....
Nice to meet you.

A: Nice to ....
too, ...

Manners matter!

How to greet someone properly

When you meet someone for the first time, greet them properly. Give a warm smile. Look at them when you speak to them. Repeat their name when you say, 'Nice to meet you.'

Saying it right

Art Integration NEP

D1. *Sing* 1.6

Listen and sing along.

S...*s*...sweets I want,
T...*t*...tarts and jam;
P...*p*...pick the tarts first,
N...*n*...now lick the jam.

D2. *Repeat*

Listen and repeat the words aloud. Pay attention to the beginning sound of each word.

sat	sun	six	sit
tap	tin	top	tub
pat	pan	pin	pot
nip	nag	net	nut

D3. *Sort*

Say these words aloud. Circle the word in each row that does not begin with the same sound.

sat	cat	set	sap	sip
pan	tan	pot	pit	pat
tap	nap	nab	nib	nun
top	tip	sat	ten	tag

D4. *Identify*

Say these words aloud. Underline the common sound in each word.

sat	pat	nap
bat	tap	man

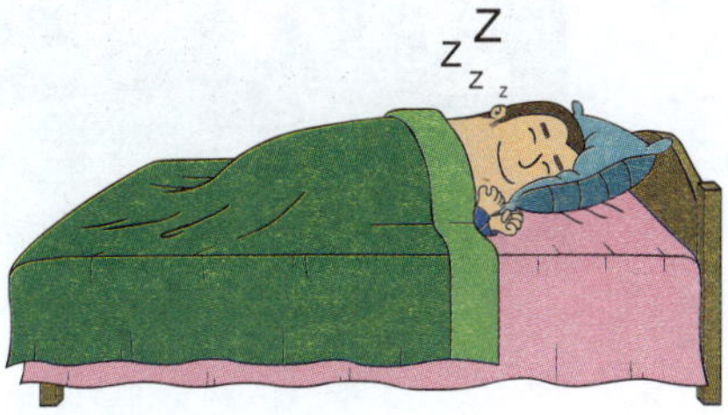

Dictation time

E. *Listen and write*

Listen to the words and write them down correctly.

1 ....

2 ....

3 ....

4 ....

5 ....

6 ....

7 ....

8 ....

Interacting and communicating

Critical Thinking NEP

F. *Look and greet*

Work in groups of four. Choose a leader. The leader will point to the pictures one by one. Greet your friends as per the time of the day. Take turns to greet.

1

2

3

4

5

Fun Activity

Collaboration NEP

Let's play a game: Catch the greeting ball.

Stand in a circle. Your teacher will give you a greeting ball. Throw the ball to a student in the circle after greeting him or her. The student will catch the ball and throw it to another student after greeting him or her.

Remember to throw it to someone new every time you get a chance.

2 Hello! My name is Raman.

In this chapter, we will:

- listen and learn to say something about ourselves.
- learn to talk about what we like.
- learn to agree with someone.
- learn to say words beginning with consonant sounds c, d, h, m, r and practise vowel sound i.

Getting started

Critical Thinking NEP

A. *Identify* **Look at the pictures. Tick (✓) only the ones in which people are meeting. Do not tick those in which people are saying goodbye.**

1 

2 

3 

4 

Listening and learning

B1. *Listen*

2.1

Listen to Raman. What is he talking about?

B2. *Gap-fill*

2.2

Listen again. What does Raman say? Fill in the table.

Name (write full name)	
Age	
Class	
Lives in	
Likes	

B3. *Match*

2.3

Sanvi and Adi meet each other for the first time. They tell each other about themselves. Listen to them talk and match the things with the correct person.

Speaking and practising

C1. *Introduce* — Look at this example.

Communication Skills NEP

Manners matter!

How to introduce yourself properly

When you meet someone for the first time, stand up to meet them. Give a warm smile. It makes them feel welcome. Be warm and polite. Shake hands or fold your hands in greeting, as in namaste. Then, introduce yourself. Say your name clearly. Nod your head when they tell you their name and respond with 'Nice to meet you.'

Now work in pairs. Greet each other. Then, talk about yourself.

A: Hello! My name is ....
I'm .... years old. I study in Class ....

B: Hello, ... ! My name is .... I'm .... years old. I study in Class ....
I like .... Do you like them?

A: Yes, I like .... *(or)*
No, I do not like ....

C2. *Share*

Tell your classmates about yourself.

Saying it right

Art Integration NEP

D1. *Listen* 2.4

Listen to this poem and sing along.

I have a little cat,
I call it Molly,
It is very fat.
I have a little hen,
I call it Penny,
It is black.
We roll in the grass,
And we run in the garden,
We are best friends.

D2. *Repeat* 2.5

Listen to the words and repeat them. Pay attention to the beginning sounds of these words.

cat	car	cup	cop
hat	ham	hip	him
dam	dip	dig	dog

man	map	mill	mug
ran	rat	rip	rug

Now read the words aloud.

D3. *Say aloud*

Say these words aloud. Find them in the word grid.

rib hit map dip cap

A	C	A	P	N	E
S	W	Q	T	Y	I
M	E	P	N	K	H
A	D	H	I	T	L
P	I	C	S	R	K
S	P	G	S	J	U
F	D	R	I	N	K
G	G	R	I	B	O

Dictation time

E. *Listen and write*

DT

Listen to the words and write them down correctly.

1 .... 5 ....

2 .... 6 ....

3 .... 7 ....

4 .... 8 ....

Interacting and communicating

F1. *Gap-fill* 2.6

Listen to some people talk about themselves and fill in the blanks. Then, say aloud the complete sentences.

ball	piano	tennis	birds	toys

1. Sam likes to play ....
2. Rahul likes ....
3. Seetha likes to play the ....
4. Tina likes to play with a ....
5. Rayan likes ....

Collaboration NEP

F2. *Talk*

Listen to your teacher tell you about a few things she likes. If you also like the same thing, raise your hand and say, 'I like it too'.

Fun Activity

Critical Thinking • Art Integration NEP

Listen and solve the riddle. Colour the correct picture.

Who am I?

2.7

Hello!

I have four legs.

I have a long tail.

I like to live in the jungle.

I am the .... of the jungle.

I like to roar loudly.

I am a ....

3 This is my home.

In this chapter, we will:

- learn to talk about our family and home.
- listen and learn about the parts of a house.
- learn to describe people.
- learn to say words beginning with consonant sounds g, l, f, b and practise vowel sound a and i.

Getting started

Art Integration NEP

A. *Colour* **Look at the picture of a family. Who are these people? Colour the people who live in your house.**

Listening and learning

Critical Thinking NEP

B1. *Listen* 3.1

Listen to Mani tell you about her house. Listen to it twice. Then read the words given below for different places. Colour the happy face if her house has that place. Colour the sad face if her house does not have that place.

1. library ☺ ☹
2. garden ☺ ☹
3. pond ☺ ☹
4. kitchen ☺ ☹
5. tennis court ☺ ☹
6. bedroom ☺ ☹
7. living room ☺ ☹
8. play room ☺ ☹

B2. *Listen* 3.2

Look at this picture of Deepak's family. Listen to him carefully. He is telling you about his family. First, only listen. Then, colour each person's dress correctly.

Speaking and practising

C1. *Talk*

Paste photographs of any four of your family members here. Then, tell your friend about them.

Word Wizard: Useful words and phrases

You may use these words to describe your family.

mother	curious	tall	kind	beautiful
father	young	smart	loving	handsome
grandfather	clever	strict	happy	playful
grandmother	old	helpful	caring	pretty
brother	friendly	thin	funny	short
sister	cute	naughty	sweet	chubby

You may say:

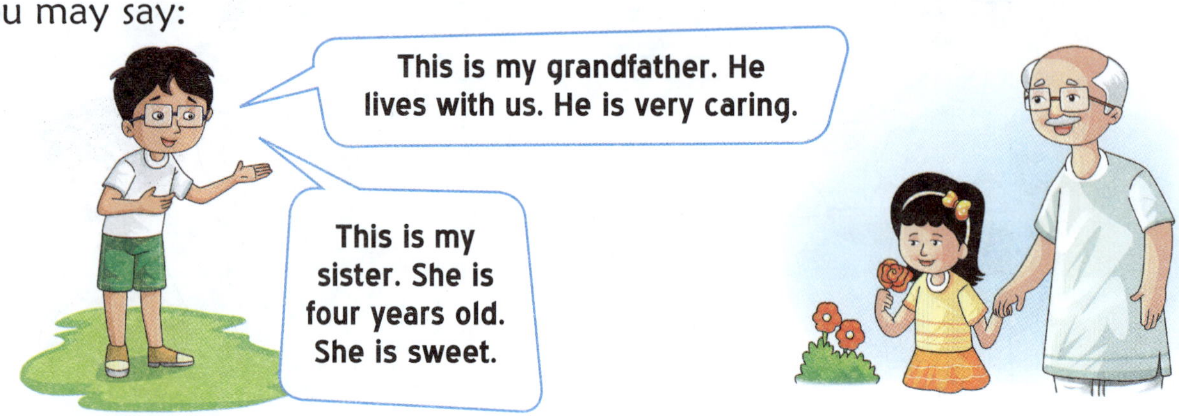

Communication Skills • Art Integration NEP

C2. *Discuss* **Work in pairs. Draw a big picture of your house on a chart paper. Take turns and tell your partner about your house. What are the things both of your houses have in common?**

Grammar Guide: Interesting language points

You may make sentences like these:

I live in an apartment/a flat/cottage/bungalow/villa.

There is a/There are .... *I have a/I have ....*

bedroom/ bedrooms	bathroom/ bathrooms	kitchen/ garden	living room/ library	dining room/ prayer room	home office	balcony	terrace	hall
in my house.								

Saying it right

Happiness Content NEP

D1. *Sing*

3.3

Listen and sing along.

The big fat lamb,
Has a fine large bag,
With a fig and grass in it;
The big fat lamb,
Eats the fig,
And bleats in glee;
Baaaaaa baaaaa,
Baa baa baa,
Baaaaaa baaaaa,
Baa baa baa.

D2. *Repeat*

3.4

Listen and repeat the words aloud.

girl	gill	gift	gate
lip	lap	leg	let
fish	fat	fin	fox
bag	bug	bill	bin

D3. *Say aloud*

Look at the things. Say their names. Add a or i to complete the words.

1 b ..... g

2 p ..... n

3 f ..... n

4 t ..... n

5 b ..... t

6 l ..... d

D4. *Say aloud*

Say aloud the words on the kites. Join the kites that begin with the same sound.

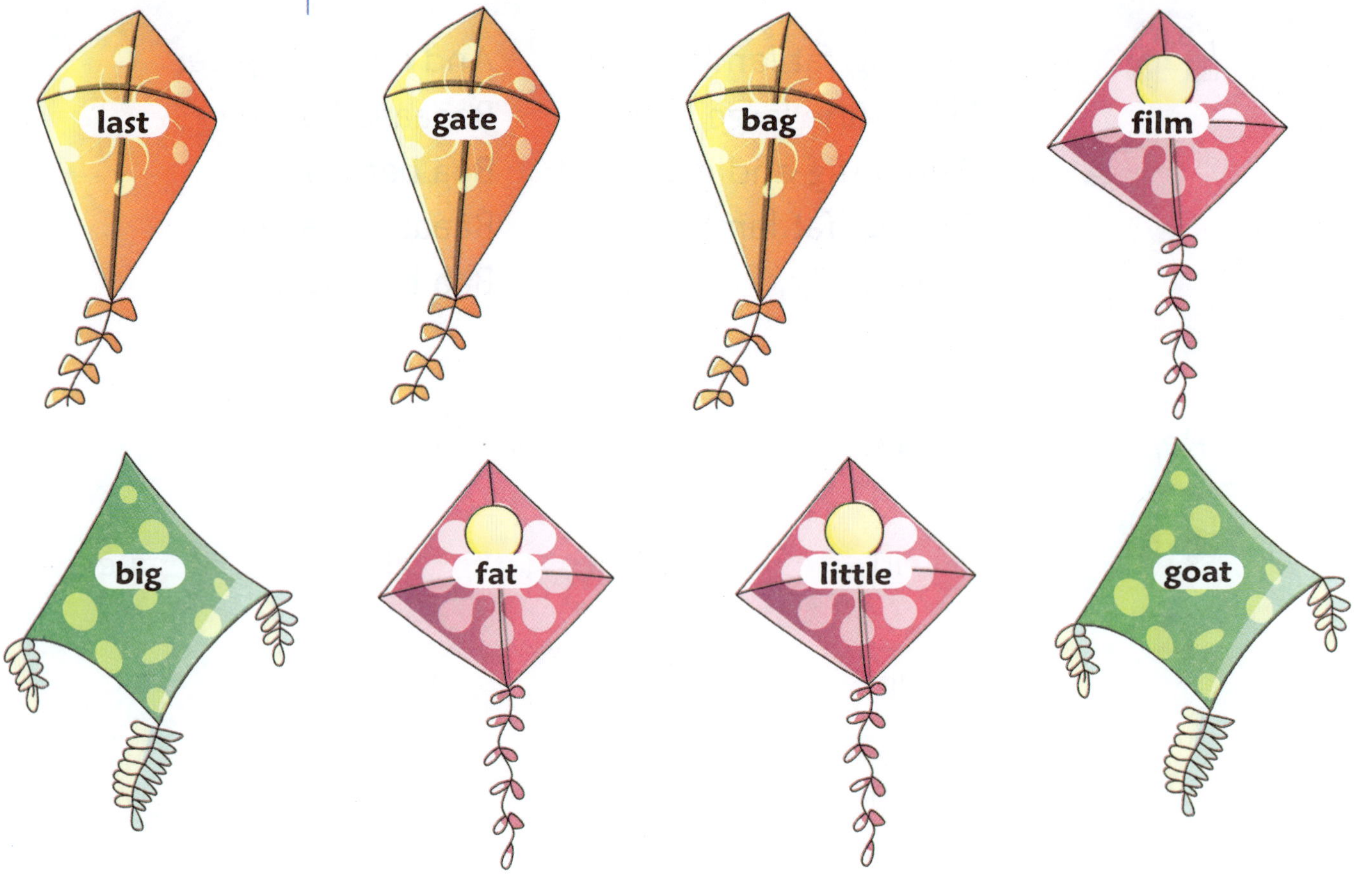

Dictation time

E. *Listen and write*

Listen to the words and write them down correctly.

1 ....

2 ....

3 ....

4 ....

5 ....

6 ....

7 ....

8 ....

Interacting and communicating

F. *Ask and answer* 3.5

Look at the picture. You will hear some questions. Listen to them carefully and answer them.

Then, in pairs, ask and answer questions about each other's family.

Grammar Guide: Interesting language points

You may use these action words in sentences to answer the questions.

playing reading dancing eating walking gardening

They are ....

He is ....

She is ....

Fun Activity

Cross-curricular NEP

Make your family tree. Draw/Paste pictures and add the names of the family members.

Take a break

A Game of Dice

Collaboration NEP

Roll the dice. Look at the picture next to the number. Say the first sound of the word.

Additional: Say another word that begins with that sound. It should not be from the picture board given below.

4 This is my friend.

In this chapter, we will:

- learn to listen for details about people.
- learn to describe a person and talk about them.
- learn to say words beginning with the consonant sounds l, m, p and practise vowel sound e.

Getting started

Happiness Content NEP

A. *Sing*

Listen to the song and sing along.

Listening and learning

B1. *Listen*

Listen to Ayan. What is he talking about?

B2. *Colour*

Listen again to what Ayan says. Colour the dresses of the children correctly.

B3. *Listen*

Listen carefully. Join the names of the children with their pictures.

1 2 3 4 5

a. Nivi   b. Izam   c. Sanjay   d. Sneha   e. Shweta

Speaking and practising

C1. *Describe*

Work in pairs. Describe your friend to your partner.

Word Wizard: Useful words and phrases

Here are some words you can use to describe your friend.

My friend is...		
tall	short	plump
handsome	pretty	slim
happy	sad	angry
shy	funny	brave
polite	smart	kind
lazy	naughty	clever

My friend has...		
long hair	short hair	curly hair
a beautiful smile	a nice smile	a lovely smile
a long nose	a small nose	a big nose

My friend wears...		
a cap	shoes	a scarf
glasses	a ponytail	earrings

Collaboration NEP

C2. *Guess*

Now form groups of four students each. Take turns to describe any student in your class. Your group has to guess the student's name.

Saying it right

D1. *Recite* 4.5

Listen and recite.

Letty the pet hen,
Met the red hen,
When she went to the wet pen;
Peg the red hen,
Pecked ten men,
Then Letty and Peg hid in the den.

D2. *Say aloud* 4.6

Listen and repeat aloud.

pen	peck	pet	peg
let	led	left	leg

men	met	mess	mesh
egg	elf	elk	elbow

Dictation time

E. *Listen and write*

Listen to the words and write them down correctly.

1 .... 5 ....

2 .... 6 ....

3 .... 7 ....

4 .... 8 ....

Interacting and communicating

Critical Thinking NEP

F1. *Sort*

Shubi has many friends. Some of them are her neighbours, and some of them study with her in school. Listen to Shubi. While you listen, draw a line joining each friend to school or home.

1 2 3 4

Communication Skills NEP

F2. **Share**

Now, tell your partner about your neighbour. Listen carefully when it is your turn to listen. Then, tell another friend what your partner told you.

Grammar Guide: Interesting language points

To talk about what your friend has told you, you may use the following:

.... has a neighbour. His/Her neighbour's name is ....

Example: Shubi has a neighbour. Her neighbour's name is Charles.

Fun Activity

Ishir has many friends. They all look different. Here are some words that can be used to describe them. Find them in the wordsearch.

small	tall	short	thin
fair	fat	dark	fit

t	a	l	l	b	z	s
w	s	h	o	r	t	m
s	l	i	n	e	h	a
f	a	t	r	f	i	l
i	f	k	e	a	n	l
t	s	d	g	i	h	j
t	e	d	a	r	k	d

5 This is my classroom.

In this chapter, we will:

- learn to talk about school and classroom.
- learn to describe things using shapes, colours and textures.
- learn to make polite requests and ask for permission.
- learn to say consonant sounds r, s, t and practise vowel sounds e and a.

Getting started

A. *Look and find*

Look at this picture and circle the things given in the box.

pencils	erasers	blackboard
notebooks	schoolbag	round stool

Listening and learning

B1. *Listen* 5.1

Listen to Alia. She is talking about her class and school.

Critical Thinking NEP

B2. *Match* 5.2

Listen to Alia again. Listen and match the words correctly.

1	desks	a.	large
2	indoor stadium	b.	rectangular
3	playground	c.	rough
4	sand	d.	wooden
5	door	e.	square

B3. *Gap-fill* 5.3

Amit is a new boy in your class. Listen to Amit asking for permission in different situations. Then, choose the correct words from the box to complete each request.

football with you	your pencil
come in	eat my lunch
sit here	have some water

1 May I .... ?

2 Can I play .... ?

3 May I .... ?

4 Can I .... ?

5 May I borrow .... ?

6 Can I .... ?

Speaking and practising

C1. *Describe*

Work in pairs. Describe your school playground to your partner.

Grammar Guide: Interesting language points

To describe the playground, you may use the following:

Our school playground is ....

It has a/an ....

It does not have a/an ....

big	small	seesaw
slide	basketball court	sandpit
grass	cricket pitch	swing

C2. *Ask and do* **Work in groups of four. Look at the pictures. Ask your friends to do the actions shown in the pictures. Take turns.**

Manners matter!

Asking for permission

When we ask for permission, we should do it politely. We should wait for our turn and ask respectfully. We must speak softly and not raise our voice.

It is good to say 'please' when you want something.

Always say 'Thank you' if you get permission to do something.

1. Ask for permission to come in.

2. Ask for permission to sit down.

3. Ask for permission to borrow a book.

4. Ask for permission to drink water.

Saying it right

D1. *Repeat* 5.4

Listen to these sentences. Repeat them slowly.

The rabbit ran in the rain for a raw radish.

Sam slips slowly spilling some sweet and sour soup.

Ten taps fill ten tanks.

D2. *Say aloud*

Listen to the words. Then, say them aloud. Pay attention to the beginning sound of these words.

rat	red	rag	rest	rent
sap	sell	sip	soap	see
tap	tip	top	tell	test

D3. *Say aloud*

Look at the pictures and say their names. Fill in the missing letters to complete the words.

1 

l ..... g

2 

r ..... t

3 

h ..... t

4 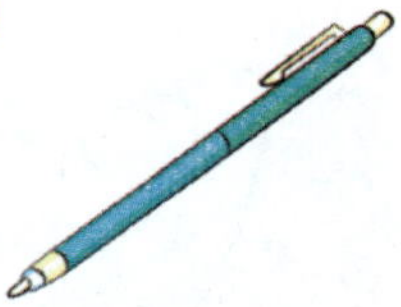

p ..... n

5 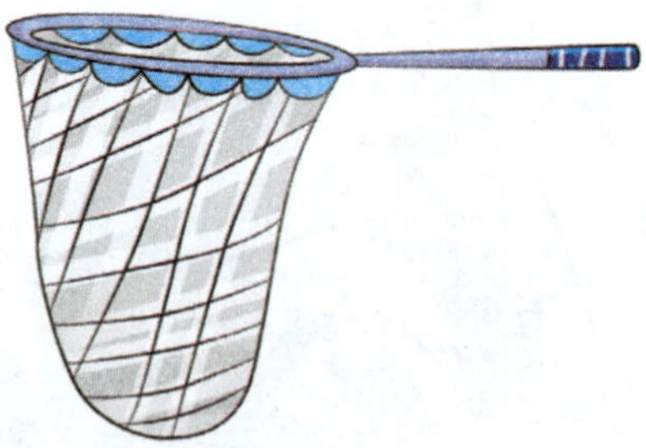

n ..... t

6 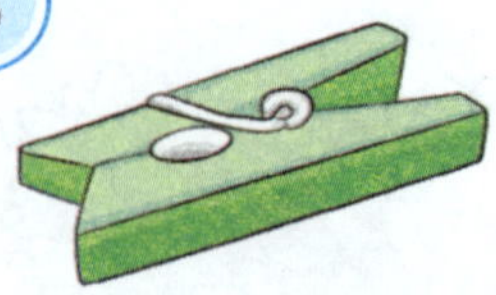

p ..... g

What sounds do the letters in the blanks make?

D4. *Draw* — **Help Alia reach the playground. Follow the words with the e sound, as in *rest* and *sell*.**

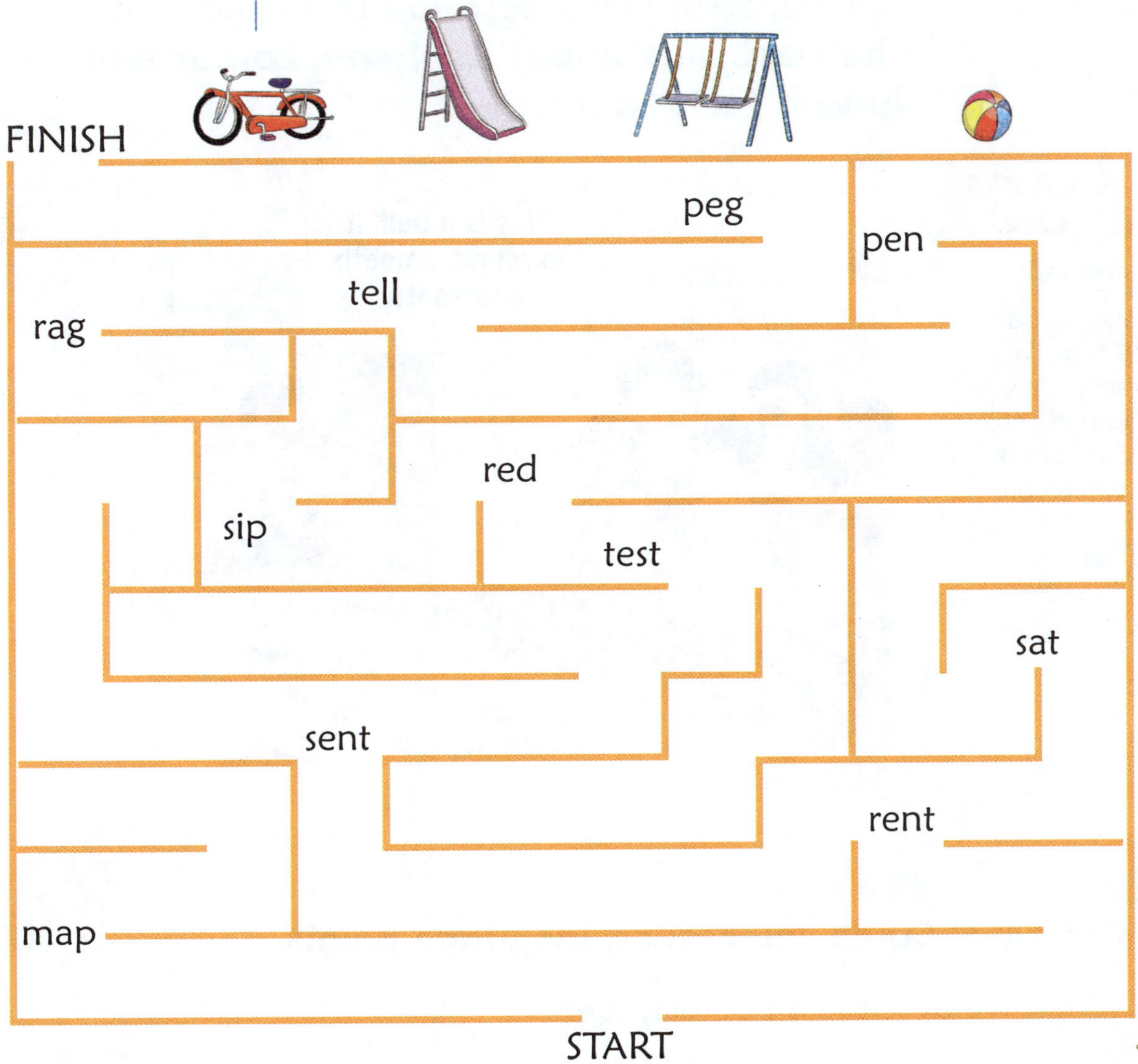

Dictation time

E. *Listen and write* — **Listen to the words and write them down correctly.**

1 .... 5 ....

2 .... 6 ....

3 .... 7 ....

4 .... 8 ....

Interacting and communicating

F1. *Show and tell* **Choose a simple object and bring it to school. Show and describe this object to the class. Talk about its shape, colour and how it feels to touch.**

Manners matter!

Show and tell

Greet and introduce yourself first. Then, with a smile on your face, show the object to the class. Speak clearly when you describe it.

Grammar Guide: Interesting language points

When we describe an object, we:

- talk about what it looks like.
- describe its size, colour and shape.
- talk about the material it is made of and its use. We can also say how it feels to touch.

When we describe an object, we say,

This is a .... It is .... It is made of ....
We use it for ....

For example: This is a pencil. It is long and hard. It is made of wood. We use it for writing.

F2. *Ask*

Ask for your teacher's permission to do the following things.

- go to the washroom/library/playground
- drink water
- enter the classroom
- borrow a pencil

Fun Activity

Find five differences in the two pictures and share them with your class.

6 I have a pet.

In this chapter, we will:

- listen and learn about animals and birds.
- listen and learn to describe actions using the *-ing* form of verbs.
- learn to talk about pets and how to take care of them.
- learn to say words with consonant sounds s, t, n, p and practise vowel sound i.

Getting started

Cross-curricular NEP

A. *Identify*

Look at the shadows. Can you say the names of these birds and animals?

When you have an answer, *say:*
The first one is a ....

1

2

3

4

5

6

Listening and learning

B1. *Listen*

6.1

Listen to Kanav and Swati.
Where are they going?

B2. *Listen and mark*

6.2

Listen again to Kanav and Swati. Tick (✓) the actions that they talk about.

3 GOOD HEALTH AND WELL-BEING

1  ☐

2  ☐

3  ☐

4  ☐

5  ☐

6  ☐

7  ☐

8  ☐

9  ☐

10  ☐

Cross-curricular NEP

B3. *Listen and write* 6.3

Rina's teacher is telling them about wild and pet animals and what they need. Listen and write the names of the animals in the correct columns.

Wild animals	Pet animals

What are the four things all animals need to be happy?

B4. *Listen* 6.4

Listen to Nirmal talking about his dog.

Speaking and practising

Communication Skills NEP

C1. *Ask and answer*

Work in small groups of four. Ask your friends what they do in the park. Your friends may answer the question with the help of the words in the box. Take turns.

Word Wizard: Useful words and phrases

Here are some words to help you.

play	swing	slide	run
meet friends	eat	walk	exercise

Experiential Learning • Happiness Content NEP

C2. *Talk* 6.5

Look at the pictures of the children with their pets. They take care of their pets in different ways. Listen to them. Now, tell your friends how you take/would take care of your pets.

1 

2 

3 

4

5

6

Word Wizard: Useful words and phrases

Here are some words to help you.

feed	clean	play with	give milk/water
walk	take care	bathe	love

Saying it right

D1. *Recite*

6.6

Listen to this poem and learn to recite it.

Ten tin men with their ten tin pets,
The ten tin pets sit in their tin nests,
In their ten nests do the ten pets sit;
With ten tin men sit ten tin pets.

D2. *Say aloud*

6.7

Listen and repeat. Pay attention to the ending sound in each word.

pen	ten	tin	bin
tap	nap	sip	nip

bus	yes	gas	pus
cat	pat	nut	but

D3. *Say and colour*

Look at this picture. Read the words aloud. Identify the words that end in t sound and colour them yellow. All other words must be coloured red.

Dictation time

E. *Listen and write*

DT

Listen to the words and write them down correctly.

1 ....

2 ....

3 ....

4 ....

5 ....

6 ....

7 ....

8 ....

Interacting and communicating

Communication Skills NEP

F1. *Discuss* **Work in groups of four. Do you have a pet? If yes, talk about it. If you don't have a pet, imagine the one you would like to have and talk about it.**

Word Wizard: Useful words and phrases

Which pet do you have?	What is its name?
What does it look like?	What does it eat?
What does it do every day?	

Critical Thinking NEP

F2. *Talk* 6.8 **Look at the picture. The children are playing in the park. Listen to the questions. Say 'Yes, they do' if they are doing the action. Say 'No, they don't' if they are not doing the action.**

Fun Activity

Collaboration • Cross-curricular NEP

Play a game in groups of four. One of you will make an animal sound. The rest of the group will guess the animal. Take turns. Follow the example.

Take a break

Art Integration NEP

Word Bee

Colour the bee by the beginning sound of each word. Follow the key.

s - orange | b - blue | m - green | l - yellow
c - purple | d - red | t - pink | p - white

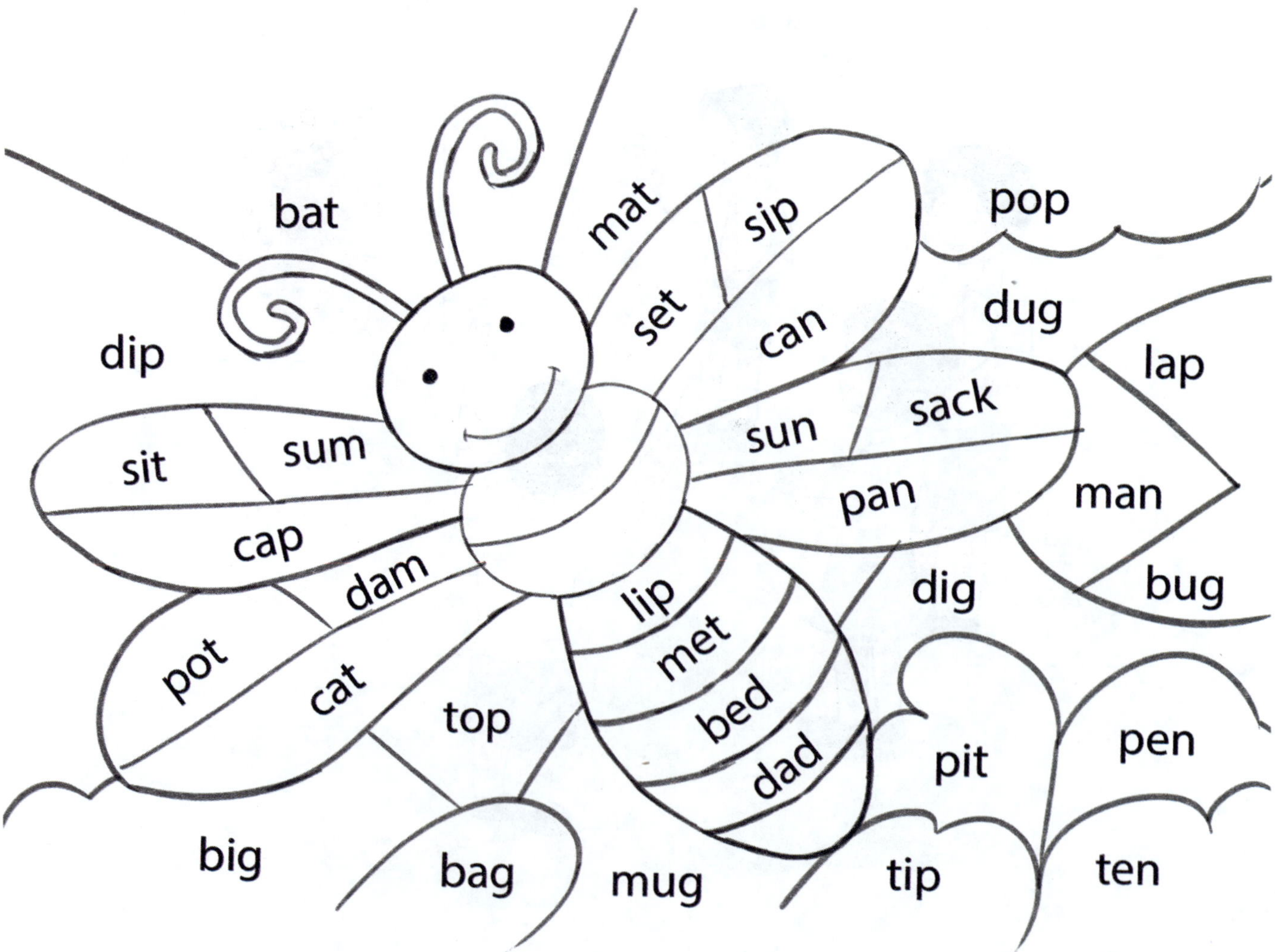

After colouring the picture, read the words aloud.

7 I like to dance and play.

In this chapter, we will:

- learn to talk about different places at school.
- learn to express our likes and dislikes.
- learn to say words ending in consonant sounds ck, m, d and practise vowel sound o.

Getting started

Happiness Content NEP

A. *Sing* 7.1 — **Listen to the song and sing along.**

Listening and learning

B1. *Listen* 7.2 — **Listen to Tanshi and Kartik talk about the places they like in school.**

B2. *Sort*

7.3

Listen again. Write K for the places Kartik likes. Write T for the places Tanshi likes.

B3. *Choose*

7.4

Listen to Divya speaking about what she likes to do. You can see three options. Choose the correct option to complete the sentences.

Divya likes to 	pray	dance and play	eat sweets	in the morning.
	sleep	play with a ball	study	at school.
	read a book	share lunch with a friend	play on the swings	during the lunch break.
	take a shower	watch TV	eat an ice cream	at home.

Speaking and practising

Communication Skills NEP

C1. *Tell and share*

Work with a partner. Tell your partner about a thing that you like to eat and a thing that you don't like to eat.

Word Wizard: Useful words and phrases

You may choose from the food items given in the box.

pizza	chips	biscuits	pumpkins	carrots
apples	burgers	milk	eggs	sweets
ladies' fingers	brinjals	tomatoes	oranges	grapes

C2. *List and talk* **In your mind, make a list of three food items that you like and don't like. Tell your classmates about them.**

Saying it right

Art Integration NEP

D1. *Listen* 7.5 **Listen to the rhyme and sing along.**

Tick tock, tick tock,
Hickory dickory dock,
The mouse ran up the clock;
The clock struck one,
The mouse ran down,
Hickory dickory dock.

Pay attention to the sound made by the letters ck.

D2. *Repeat*

Listen and repeat these words aloud. Pay attention to the sound made by the highlighted letters.

frock	flock	sick	neck
rod	god	cod	pod
mum	sum	rim	gum

D3. *Look and say*

Look at the pictures and say their names aloud. What is the common sound in these words?

1 
dog

2 
log

3 
cot

4 
pot

D4. *Say aloud*

Look at the pictures and say what they are. Complete the words ending in ck. Then read the words aloud.

1  ....ck

2  ....ck

3  ....ck

4 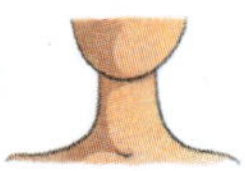 ....ck

5  ....ck

6  ....ck

Dictation time

E. *Listen and write*

Listen to the words and write them down correctly.

1 ....

2 ....

3 ....

4 ....

5 ....

6 ....

7 ....

8 ....

Interacting and comunicating

Communication Skills NEP

F1. *Talk*

Your teacher will ask you some questions about your likes and dislikes. Listen to the questions and answer them.

F2. *Listen* 7.7

Listen to David talking about his favourite things. Tick (✓) the things he likes. Draw a cross (✗) on the things he does not like.

1. For breakfast

2. Go to school by

3. In the evening

4. On Sunday

Fun Activity

Cross-curricular • Art Integration NEP

Colour the things that you like from the pictures given below.

8 I feel happy.

In this chapter, we will:

- learn to express our feelings and needs.
- learn to offer food or drinks.
- learn to accept or reject an offer politely.
- learn to say words with consonant sounds y, w, z and practise vowel sounds o and i.

Getting started

Art Integration NEP

A. *Look and draw* — **Look at the pictures. Draw and make one face look happy, one look sad, and one look angry.**

Listening and learning

B1. *Listen* 8.1 — **Listen to some people talk about how they feel.**

B2. *Match* 8.2

Listen to the talk again. Match the children with what they need.

Shafiq	needs a sweater.
Anna	needs to drink water.
Naman	needs to eat food.
Niti	needs to rest.
Arvind	needs to switch on the fan.

B3. *Listen and mark* 8.3

Listen to the conversation. Hema is feeling hungry and thirsty. Tick (✓) the pictures of the food she likes. Put a cross (✗) on the pictures of the food she does not like.

☐

☐

☐

☐

☐

☐

Speaking and practising

Communication Skills NEP

C1. *Ask*

Work in pairs. Talk to your partner. Offer food or drinks to him or her by asking, 'Do you want...?' Take turns and ask at least three questions.

Manners matter!

Offering food

When we offer food to someone, we do so politely and with respect.

Accepting or rejecting food

When we accept or reject food, we use please and thank you. We say: Yes, please or No, thank you.
It is usually polite to accept a little to show respect.

You may use these words to ask the questions.

water	pizza	noodles	fruits
juice	cake	bread	apple
milk	banana		

C2. *Talk*

Tell your friend how you are feeling right now.

Word Wizard: Useful words and phrases

You may use these words:

angry
excited
happy
sleepy
hungry

I feel ....

thirsty
cold
hot
tired

Saying it right

D1. *Repeat* 8.4

Listen to the tongue twister and repeat it.

Can you walk in a zigzag way to the zoo?

D2. *Say aloud* 8.5

Listen and say the words aloud.

yes	yet	yap	yell	yesterday
wag	work	wick	well	wood
zig	zag	zen	zip	zoo

Critical Thinking • Art Integration NEP

D3. *Say and colour*

Look at the pictures. Say what they are. Colour the picture yellow if its name begins with y sound. Colour it brown if its name begins with w sound and blue if it begins with z sound.

D4. *Identify*

Read and say the words aloud in each row. What is the common sound in them?

pit	hit	tip	dig
pot	hot	top	dog

Can you add two more words to each row with the same sound?

Dictation time

E. *Listen and write*

Listen to the words and write them down correctly.

1 .... 5 ....

2 .... 6 ....

3 .... 7 ....

4 .... 8 ....

Interacting and communicating

F1. *Listen*

Sania and Manish are having lunch at a restaurant with their mother. Tick (✓) the things they order.

Collaboration NEP

F2. *Enact* **Form small groups and enact a scene at a restaurant. Decide the things you would like to eat. One person in the group may take down the order and serve.**

Word Wizard: Useful words and phrases

You may use the following sentences:

Student A: Would you like to have .... ?

Student B: Yes, I would like to have ....

No, I do not like .... I will have ....

Communication Skills NEP

F3. *Express* **Read the situations given below. Tell your friends how you feel in these situations.**

Word Wizard: Useful words and phrases

I win a match.	I am late.
I eat well.	I sleep well.
I study.	I play.
I help my family.	I go to school.
I ride my bicycle.	It rains.
It is dark.	I see a puppy.

Fun Activity

Cross-curricular NEP

Sing this song with actions.

8.7

Sometimes on my face, you'll see, *(point to the face)*

How I feel inside of me. *(point to the chest)*

A smile means happy, *(smile)*

A frown means sad. *(frown)*

And gritting teeth, means I'm mad. *(grit your teeth)*

When I'm proud, I beam and glow, *(smile wide)*

But when I'm sorry, my head hangs low. *(bow your head)*

Look at Hema's different faces. Can you tell how she is feeling in each of them?

1 ....

2 ....

3 ....

9 Where is my schoolbag?

In this chapter, we will:

- learn to talk about common places.
- learn to listen and follow directions.
- learn to ask for and give directions.
- learn to say words with consonant sounds d, g, n, p, t and practise vowel sound u.

Getting started

Happiness Content NEP

A. *Listen* 9.1 — **Listen and move along.**

Listening and learning

B1. *Listen* 9.2 — **Listen to Rima give directions about how to go from her house to the school.**

Critical Thinking NEP

B2. *Listen and follow* 9.3

Listen to Rima again and follow her directions on the map.

B3. *Listen and match* 9.4

Ajit is new to school. Arpita is helping him find the different places in the school. Match each room with the place near it.

The office is near the	sick room.
The canteen is near the	playground.
The toilet is next to the	teacher's room.
The library is opposite the	dance class.

Speaking and practising

Communication Skills NEP

C1. *Talk*

Work in pairs. Take turns and tell your partner where these places are in your school.

library canteen dance room bookshop

Manners matter!

Giving directions

When we tell someone directions to a place, we do so properly. Speak clearly and slowly. Point the directions with your hands. Ask questions to check whether the listener has understood your directions. If you don't know where the place is, say, I am sorry, I don't know. Do not give wrong directions.

You may use these directions:

It is next to the ....

It is opposite ....

It is near the ....

C2. *Role-play*

Read the dialogues with your friend. Practise saying them.

A: Where are the children?

B: They are in the classroom.

A: Where is their teacher?

B: He is in the library.

A: Where are the notebooks?

B: They are in the cupboard.

A: Where are the lunch boxes?

B: They are on the shelf.

C3. *Practise*

Now, work in pairs. Ask more questions and answer them in the same way.

Saying it right

D1. *Say aloud*

9.5

Listen to the tongue twister. Try to say it fast.

The mutt dug the bug up from the mud.

D2. *Repeat*

9.6

Listen to the words and repeat them. Pay attention to the ending sound in each word.

mud	bud	bug	dug
bun	sun	fun	nun
cup	pup	cap	tap
but	cut	hut	nut

Now listen to these words. Can you find the common sound in them?

up	uncle	under	umbrella

D3. *Sort*

Say these words aloud. In each set, circle the word that does not end with the same sound.

1.	duck	bud	mud
2.	lug	mug	stuck
3.	run	bug	sun
4.	cup	fun	pup
5.	bus	but	cut

Dictation time

E. *Listen and write*

Listen to the words and write them down correctly.

1 .... 5 ....

2 .... 6 ....

3 .... 7 ....

4 .... 8 ....

Interacting and communicating

F1. *Look and point at*

Look at the picture. Your teacher will ask you where the things are. Point at the things, and answer in a sentence.

You can say, '*It is* ....'.

Word Wizard: Useful words and phrases

Here are some words to help you.

on	in	under	near	next to	opposite
the window	the cupboard	the table	the blackboard	the door	the desk

Communication Skills NEP

F2. *Talk* **Now, tell your friends where you keep your favourite things in your room.**

Fun Activity

Art Integration NEP

9.7 **Listen to the Hokey Pokey song and do the actions.**

TAKE a break

India Focus NEP

Majestic Monuments

Match the pictures with the beginning sounds of these monuments.

g

r

l

t

j

Can you say the names of these monuments? Have you visited them already?

10 What is the time now?

In this chapter, we will:

- learn to describe the weather and tell time.
- learn to express how we feel in different kinds of weather.
- learn to ask and answer questions about daily activities.
- say words with consonant sounds g and n and practise vowel sounds o and u.

Getting started

Critical Thinking NEP

A. *Look and say* — **Look at the pictures of some places. Say which is sunny, cold, hot or rainy.**

1

2

3

4

Listening and learning

B1. *Listen*

10.1

Listen to a group of children talk about the weather of the place they live in.

Cross-curricular NEP

B2. *Listen and match*

10.2

Listen to the children again. Fill in the blanks with the correct option from the brackets. Match the sentences with the pictures.

a. 

b. 

c. 

d. 

1. This is .... (Kochi/Kullu). It rains a lot here.
2. This is .... (Delhi/Kullu). It gets really cold here.
3. This is .... (Delhi/Hyderabad). It gets really hot here.
4. This is .... (Bengaluru/Kochi). It is neither hot nor cold here.

B3. *Listen and mark* (10.3)

Listen to these people talk about time. They are talking about when they will do something. Listen to them and tick (✓) the correct time.

1. Go to school at eight o'clock/ nine o'clock	2. Have lunch at twelve o'clock/ one o'clock	3. Go home at four o'clock/ three o'clock
4. Go to play at five o'clock/ six o'clock	5. Have dinner at six o'clock/ eight o'clock	6. Sleep at eight o'clock/ nine o'clock

Speaking and practising

Communication Skills NEP

C1. *Talk*

Work in pairs. Tell your friend about the weather of the place you went for a holiday. Take turns.

Word Wizard: Useful words and phrases

You may use the words in the box.

hot

cold

rainy

dry

windy

C2. *Talk*

Work in pairs. Tell your friend at what time you wake up on Sundays.

Grammar Guide: Interesting language points

When we talk about time, we say:

What is the time now?

It is twelve o'clock.

We use at before the exact time word.

I wake up at six o'clock. I eat at eight o'clock. I go to school at half past eight.

When we talk about a longer period of time, we use in with the time period.

I wake up in the morning. I eat lunch in the afternoon.

I play in the evening. But, I sleep at night!

When we talk about days, we use on with the name of the day.

I go for a picnic on Sundays. I go to school on Mondays.

Saying it right

D1. *Sing* 10.4

Listen to the song and sing along.

Look, there's a bug,
Sitting on a nut.
Is it a slug?
Is it in the sun?
Take it in a mug,
and put it away!

D2. *Say aloud* 10.5

Listen and repeat aloud.

dog	bog	cog	fog
dug	bug	rug	lung
bun	fun	sun	gun
on	off	office	octopus

D3. *Say and sort*

Read these sets of words aloud. Underline the words that do not belong to the group.

dog	log	sag	dot
cop	ran	man	pan
dug	bug	tag	rug
sun	fun	bug	run

Dictation time

E. *Listen and write* DT

Listen to the words and write them down correctly.

1 ....

2 ....

3 ....

4 ....

5 ....

6 ....

7 ....

8 ....

Interacting and communicating

F1. *Listen and order* 10.6

Listen to Dina talk about what she does every day. Listen to her carefully and put the pictures in the correct order.

F2. *Ask*

Work in groups of four. Take turns to ask each other these questions. Use the answer prompts to form your answers.

When do you wake up?	I wake up at ....
When do you go to school?	I go to school at ....
When do you eat lunch?	I eat lunch at ....
When do you play?	I play at ....
When do you sleep?	I sleep at ....

F3. *Talk*

Look at the pictures. Your teacher will point at one picture. Tell your class about the weather in that picture. Use the words from the box to describe.

hot and dry	cold and windy
wet and cold	cold and snowy

Fun Activity

Art Integration NEP

Match the actions with the time you do them. If you don't do some of these, draw your own actions and match.

11 I can dance.

In this chapter, we will:

- learn to talk about our ability to do something using can and cannot.
- learn to ask for permission using can.
- learn to say words with long and short vowel sounds i and o.

Getting started

Happiness Content NEP

A. *Sing* 11.1

Listen and sing along.

Listening and learning

B1. *Listen*

Razak and Mina are talking. Listen to them and say what they are talking about.

Critical Thinking NEP

B2. *Listen and identify*

Listen to Razak and Mina again. Tick (✓) what the children can do.

B3. *Listen and mark* 11.4

Rayan is talking about what different animals can and cannot do. Listen carefully and tick (✓) the actions that each animal can do. Put a cross (✗) on the actions they cannot do.

	fly	hop	carry	swim	slide	walk	run	lay eggs	eat grass
	☐	☐	☐	☐	☐	☐	☐	☐	☐
	☐	☐	☐	☐	☐	☐	☐	☐	☐
	☐	☐	☐	☐	☐	☐	☐	☐	☐
	☐	☐	☐	☐	☐	☐	☐	☐	☐
	☐	☐	☐	☐	☐	☐	☐	☐	☐
	☐	☐	☐	☐	☐	☐	☐	☐	☐
	☐	☐	☐	☐	☐	☐	☐	☐	☐

Speaking and practising

C1. *Ask and answer*

Work in pairs. Ask your partner what he/she can do. Take turns to ask and answer the questions.

Word Wizard: Useful words and phrases

You may use the words in the box.

read	hop	run	climb a tree
swim	sing	dance	cook
play the piano	make a kite	clean shoes	

C2. *Discuss*

Work in small groups. Talk about what you can do that no one else can.

Saying it right

D1. *Repeat* (11.5)

Listen to the tongue twister and repeat it.

The ship with the six sheep shakes but keeps the six sheep safe.

D2. *Say aloud* (11.6)

Listen to the words and repeat them aloud. Then read the words on your own.

hill	fill	ship	slip
heel	feel	sheep	keep
stop	hop	hot	flock
droop	hoop	hoot	boot

D3. *Say aloud*

Say aloud the words in this picture.
How many words have the e sound?

in
act
eat
ill
easy
inch

tip
if
eel
win
ant
bill

ate bin mill ship and spin

Dictation time

E. *Listen and write*

DT

Listen to the words and write them down correctly.

1 ....
2 ....
3 ....
4 ....
5 ....
6 ....
7 ....
8 ....

Interacting and communicating

F1. *Listen* 11.7

Listen to Arjun tell you about the things he can do and cannot do.

Collaboration NEP

F2. *Ask and mark*

Now, work in a group. Ask three people what they can/cannot do. Write your friends' names in the table. Tick (✓) what each friend can do. Put a cross (✗) for something that they cannot do.

Action	Name	Can do	Cannot do
skate			
sing			
climb a tree			
play football			
swim			

Fun Activity

Cross-curricular NEP

11.8 **Listen to this poem. Then, read the poem along with your teacher.**

I can bark like a dog.	Woofwoof
I can moo like a cow.	Moooooooooooo
I can roar like a lion.	Roooooooar
I can hiss like a snake.	Sssssssssssssssssss
I can mew like a cat.	Meeeeeeowwwwwwww
I can quack like a duck.	Quack quack quack
I can crow like a cock.	Cocccccckadoooodledooo
I can bleat like a goat.	Baaaaaabaaaaaa

Saying it better!

Common mistakes	Use this instead
I *has* a pet dog.	I *have* a pet dog.
She *have* a headache.	She *has* a headache.
My mother *drive* a car.	My mother *drives* a car.
They *was looking* at the birds.	They *were looking* at the birds.
We *was making* a card.	We *were making* a card.
You *was asking* him a question.	You *were asking* him a question.
They *gone* to the library.	They *went* to the library.
We *goed* to the mall.	We *went* to the mall.

Common phrases

When we meet someone:

When we talk about what we like:

When we ask for permission:

When someone helps us:

Children's Literary Fest

Creativity · Art Integration NEP

Dress up as your favourite character from a story you have recently read. Then, introduce yourself to the class as that character.

Here's an example: